BREATHING
IN
BROKEN SPACES

Belinda Daou

Illustrated and Designed by
Belinda Daou

Published by Lines in Emotions Publishing

Cover Design by Belinda Daou

Interior Design and Illustrations by Belinda Daou

ISBN: 979-8-218-61921-3

First Edition: 2025

Printed in the United States of America

Disclaimer

This book is a work of poetry and creative expression. Some pieces may be inspired by real-life experiences, but names, characters, and events are used fictitiously where necessary. Any resemblance to actual persons, living or dead, is purely coincidental.

For permissions, inquiries, or more information, contact:

belinda.daou1@gmail.com

Follow the author on Instagram: @bell.d.poet

Dear Reader,

This book is a home for every feeling that once had nowhere else to go. It is made of quiet heartbreaks, whispered goodbyes, the weight of memory, and the slow, aching process of healing.

I wrote these poems in the spaces between what was and what will be. In the nights where I carried too much, in the mornings where I tried to let go. Some of these words are stitched together with love; others are held together by the remnants of something that no longer exists. They are messy, unfiltered, and real—just like grief, just like love, just like being human.

If you have ever loved someone who changed before your eyes, if you have ever held onto the past too tightly, if you have ever found yourself caught in the space between survival and hope—then I hope these pages remind you that you are not alone.

You are allowed to grieve what could have been. You are allowed to feel everything that broke you and still love yourself. You are allowed to heal at your own pace.

Thank you for holding these words with me.

With Love,

Belinda

Contents

Loving in Broken Spaces:

Trauma in Broken Spaces:

Self-Reflecting in Broken Spaces:

LOVING
IN
BROKEN SPACES

What if I missed him so much
and it never went away?

How do I break the news to my heart?
How do I say—

His face will always live
in your heart's cage,
a silent echo,
forever replayed.

A prisoner of love,
never to escape.

-What If?

I've been through letters and numbers
through science and physics
through psychology and spirituality—
I still can't understand
what you mean to me

you defy every equation
break every law of gravity

a force I can't explain
yet you pull me endlessly

I tried to find answers in the stars
in books
in the spaces between
but no theory
no belief
can define this feeling unseen

maybe some things can't be solved
not by mind
but only by heart

you'll forever be the mystery
I'm powerless
to take apart

- The Quantum of Us

Why do I choose
to see your field of flowers,
every petal glowing
with the light of what could be—

while you only see my field of weeds,
twisting,
stubborn,
fighting to bloom?

I water your beauty
with all I have,
but you pluck at my flaws,
careless with the roots
I hide beneath the soil.

Is it blindness?
Or is it love—
that I see what could grow,
while you see reasons to leave,
even the brightest of my blooms
untouched.

- Fields of Perception

You don't get to tell me
how badly you hurt me—

cracks you made,
but the pain I claim

scars you created,
but the hurt is in my name

I own the suffering,
and you own the shame

- It's Mine

It's sweet, then bitter
familiar, then suddenly strange

forever turns temporary
hope fades
as love begins to change

significant, then forgettable
a home one day, the next—
no longer mine

I build it up
only to watch it fall

maybe love
was never meant to live
between these walls

- The Architecture of Reality

I don't know
what arms have comforted you
at your weakest and lowest,

or what eyes have looked at you
hard enough to see
the softest parts of your soul.

I don't know
what feet walked miles and miles
just to be near you,

or whose hands tried
to give you everything they could.

I don't know
what hugs and kisses
have made you feel genuinely loved,

what tongues created
the most unforgettable words,

or whose lips left
marks of love on your skin.

I don't know
what hearts have loved you
deep enough to live in yours.

But I know
that this one inside my chest

would do it all again—

endlessly,
if only
to love you longer.

-You'll Miss This One Day

You are a hundred what-ifs
and maybes
a thousand potential
mornings and nights
a million possibilities
of memories we never made

but tonight—
I surrender

tonight,
I give up
I give in
I let the weight
of all our dreams slip away

my heart is tired
of chasing futures
that never seem to stay

so tonight,
my white flag flies

not in defeat
but in release

letting go
of what could've been
so I can finally
find some peace

- *White Flag*

I forgave you
as quickly as the sun
can kiss my skin

it was like choosing
to sit beneath its glare for hours,
knowing the fire
would crawl beneath my skin—

a lesson I knew
I was going to regret learning

I chose to love you,
even if my eyes had a view
of all your uncharted waters
hidden beneath your dark sea

but the hurt
of losing all of you
was far greater
than the hurt
of you hurting me

- Love & Hurt Became the Same

Love doesn't knock on your door
and wait for you to open

it kicks down the door
and sits in your house—
uninvited

-Home Invasion

If you weren't ready to lose me,
you shouldn't have walked away
faster than your heart could follow

you left shadows
where your love once stood,
your footsteps echoing
louder than your promises

did you think I wouldn't notice?
that your silence would fill the space
where your courage should have been?

if you weren't ready to lose me,
you shouldn't have let your fear
outrun the truth of what we were

- How a Coward Loves

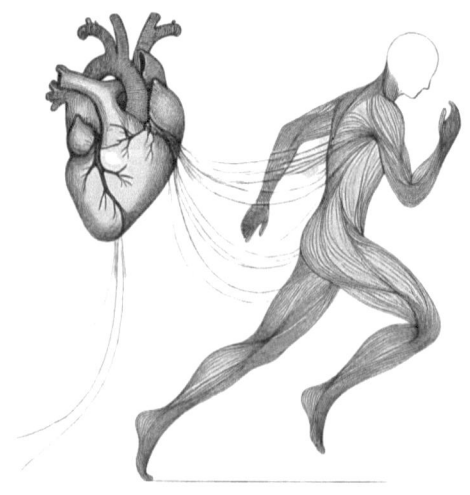

You always forget who I am
and I always remember who you were

how cruel it is,
this dance of memory and loss

where I carry the weight
of what was
while you let everything
I became for you
slip so easily away

- Your Amnesia isn't Fair

All the kissing
guessing who your heart is missing

all the encounters
your arms around her
whispering words
you swore were mine

I'll watch and bleed
I'll sew and heal
enduring pain
I shouldn't feel

you're moving on
you play the part—
but tell me it's not real

tell me they're all just a start
a story that won't transcend

as long as my name
is still tatted on your heart,
I'll find a way to pretend

-What Does the Ink on Your Heart Say?

Though I no longer know
what it feels like
between your arms

I only know—

it's still the best feeling
in the world

no touch has matched it
no warmth replaced it

and even in its absence,
it holds me tighter
than anything else ever could

-*Warmth Even in Absence*

Rearrange your words,
pull them from the wreckage—

of everything unsaid,
of everything said too harshly

maybe if you find the right ones,
you can stitch the silence back together
fill the cracks
where love slipped through

maybe
you can still save this—

before your silence
becomes the only thing I can hear

-Words Can Change Hearts

Let me dive deep,
into the waters you hide from the world

where the currents of your fears run wild,
and the shadows of your flaws linger unseen

I want to explore
the depths you keep buried—

to find the cracks,
the wounds,
the places you've long abandoned

I want to love you
where you hate yourself

to show you the beauty in the broken,
to remind you
that even the deepest scars
are worth holding onto

-You see Black, I see Gold

I want to live in a world
where I am your moon and stars—

the light
through your darkest nights

a world where my orbit
is tethered to your gravity

and even in silence,
in the dead of night,
no matter where we exist
on this spinning planet,

your eyes would still rise to find me,
anchored in your sky

- A Sky Where I Belong to You

If only I could throw up
every memory of you—

your face
your voice
your existence

scrub you from places
you've entered
that even I can't reach

spit you out,
rip you from my skin,
until there is nothing of you
left inside me

I need to be ruthless with this—
I need to cut you out,
erase you

because if you exist,
I will love you forever

and forever
will destroy me

and still,
even in my ruin,
you will live on

- A Love I Couldn't Kill

19

A silent love
eventually
loses its will
to speak

- Muted Love

I wanted you—
I still do.

even after you left,
I wanted you,
and that never faded away.

but something else grew:
a longing for a love
that chooses to stay.

you brought chaos,
left pain scattered
like shards of glass,
and walked away.

I want you to be the one for me,
but it's simpler
than I let myself believe—

if you were the one,
you simply
would have stayed.

- I Ran Out of Excuses for You

I could've been anything—
a star, a storm, a whole sky—
but I chose to be just for him

why did I crave to be small
in a world so wide?

maybe because I spent my life
breaking free
from places that never fit my soul.

he felt like something rare—
a hidden gem,
a home,
built just for me.

-I Didn't Need the World, I Needed a Home

Everything
burned brighter
when forgiveness lingered between us—

a fragile warmth
I hoped could hold forever

but the moment your eyes hardened,
forgiveness slipped
quietly
through the cracks of our roof

the lights went dark
the world turned hollow,
cold

and I knew:
we were already over.

-*Where Love Freezes*

The day you break up is the day you truly meet.

everything before was a story
you both tried to believe,
painted with hope,
wrapped in the comfort of illusions.

no sweetness, no filters—
just truth,
raw and unkind.

it's then you realize,
love is not in the falling.
it's in the reckoning.

it's not the good-mood kisses,
but the angry, desperate hugs.
it's not the polished love story,
but the hands piecing it together—
bleeding,
shaking,
refusing to let it shatter.

it's not the easy gestures
designed for convenience,
but the sacrifices that hurt,
the ones you carry in silence.

it's not the shared sunsets
that make it real,
but the courage to drag someone
from their darkness,
offering them the fragile light

you've managed to protect.

the day you break up is the day you truly meet.

where masks fall
and suppressed emotions scream.
when pretending no longer serves you,
and the real and the fake
stand side by side,
exposed.

trust is either enhanced
or broken.

all the fights,
the doubts,
the chaos—
the aching questions—

all the noise silences itself.

and in its place
comes clarity.

everything you needed to see.
everything you needed to know.

answered.
unmistakably,
loud and clear.

- When Love Stands Without Armor

I walked out of your love
like shoes I fell in love with
at first sight.

but the more I walked in them,
the more they hurt my feet.

-Breaking In, Breaking Out

I ran into him today.

I instantly wanted to cry
and smile at the same time.

my body shook—
as if it was trying to tell me something
my heart already knew.

his smile—
still sharp enough to cut through time—

it was so contagious,
slipped past my walls.
I felt like a fool in love again.

and for a moment,
I didn't care.
I was just happy to see him.

his eyes, once a language only we spoke,
the eyes that comforted me,
that loved me,
now hide behind unfamiliar glass.

those same eyes,
that once knew the depths of my soul,
now carry fading secrets,
frozen in a story we never finished—
a story I still feel from time to time.

we hugged—
a full embrace that caught me by surprise.

his touch felt the same,
but all I could think of
were the hugs
I'll never call mine again.

it lingered,
heavy with emotions I couldn't name,
and I wondered if he felt the same.

I tried not to look too hard,
tried not to let my gaze give away
the years my mind was peeling back:
his laugh,
his jokes,
his arms,
the way we fit effortlessly.

we stood there,
talking nonsense,
just to stretch the moment a little longer—
polite strangers with warm smiles and talking eyes,
standing under a cloud of memories,
pretending not to see
the pieces of us scattered between the words.

and as I drove home that night,
I cried—
for the what-ifs,
the what-could-have-been,

and whispered a quiet hope
that the love he chose

loves him
even more than I did

so that this ache in my heart
at least feels worth it.

-I Know You

I understand why he ran—
to love too much
is to hold a match
too close to paper.

you burn the edges,
thinking you're warming it,
until warmth
feels like suffocation.

maybe leaving
was the only way
he could save himself

from a love we both feared,
a love too intense
to ever be safe.

- The Spark Was the Warning

If I give up—
if I remove love from my life,
the equation
I always tied my happiness to—

will I forget you?

if love leaves,
will you leave with it?

maybe forgetting love exists
is the only way
to forget you.

-Love?...Never Heard of It

I don't think you ever understood
how much my fragile little heart loves you.

how it clings to the idea of you,
like it's never known another love.

how it holds every piece of who you are,
even when my pride,
my mind,
begs it to let go.

you never noticed the way it trembled,
how it whispered your name
in every quiet moment,

how it danced with joy,
celebrating you
even when you weren't near.

or how it kept breaking,
then mending itself,
just to give you another chance,
just to love you all over again.

logic doesn't live within its walls,
nor in the reckless way it beats.

it knows you
like it once lived in your chest.

it loves you
like it belonged to you before,

like it was yours
long before it was mine.

it knows you so well,
I'm afraid it might forget my name—

and only remember
its sole purpose
is to beat for you.

- But I Only Have One Heart

When you left,
did you realize
what you were asking me to do?

when you left,
you asked me to stop loving you.
to find someone else to love.
to forget how your arms felt
wrapped around my waist.

you asked me to forget
how much more I smiled
when the face I was smiling at
was yours.

you asked me to erase
all the moments I thought,
"this is too good to be true."

you asked me to stop wondering
if I had finally found the one.

you asked me to make you
the last person I should text,
to stop venting to you
when I've had a bad day.

you asked me to take my presence
and move it far from yours.

you asked me to stop thinking
about your face
when I first wake up,

to close my eyes
to the sparks we ignited
every time our eyes met.

you asked me to untie
the intricate bonds
we knotted together
day by day,
for a year.

you asked me to stop sniffing
your scent off the blankets
we once cuddled in,
to wash away every stained memory
on the clothes I wore around you.

you asked me to stop finding
strands of your hair
still scattered in my house.

you asked me to get used to saying,
"I miss him."

to stop smiling
when I say your name out loud.

you asked me to remove you
from the future
I was so excited about,
to forget the faces of the children
I imagined we'd have.

you asked me to start seeing you
as a boy instead of a man.

you asked me to go back
and dissect every word
you've ever said,
to doubt every innocent story
you've ever told.

you asked me to forget
the reasons I fell in love with you.

you asked me to wake up every day
and wonder why
I wasn't good enough for you.

to trade my smiles for tears
when I think about all our memories.

you asked me to forget
all the ways you felt about me,
to let your face fade
into a stranger's someday.

you asked me to erase your existence,
to press restart.

you asked me—
to move you

from the man of my dreams
to the list of men
who broke my heart.

-When You Left

Sometimes,
I talk to the universe about you—

whisper your name into the stars
just to feel like we still exist
in the same world,

just to pretend
the distance
isn't infinite.

- I Hope the Stars Tell You

I want to surrender to you.

let me fall—
not gently,
but completely.

let me begin
where love always breaks.

heartbreak walked beside me,
each scar a breadcrumb
leading me to this moment—
to you.

every "forever" I thought I wanted
was only temporary.

I don't want to fight anymore.

I want to burn.
I want to drown.
I want to finally surrender—

to the fire,
to the flood,
to love
in you.

- Can I Finally Relax Now?

When they say move on,
do they understand
that telling me how to feel
doesn't make my love
any less wrong in their eyes?

do they know
how many heartbeats were made
every day I fell deeper in love with you?

do they know
how many broken pieces I'm trying to fix—
living life high on glue?

if I loved you for 2,555 days,
do they want me to count
how many heartbeats multiplied and tripled
from day one until today?

if they understood how my heart loves,
words would escape them.
they wouldn't know what to say.

would that make it easier for them to see
why my limbs only move
in baby steps away from you?

I've been running from you
in slow motion,
while time slipped
from right under me
and flew away.
if they knew

what dying from heartbreak felt like,
I wouldn't need to explain.
they'd just know.

all that stubborn love
trapped in my veins, in my brain—
it's lived through many lifetimes ago.

they haven't seen your soul
through my eyes,
how the world stopped
and reduced to four walls in size,
encircled by nothing but you.

just because I love you now
in smaller waves,
it doesn't mean my heart
forgot how to love you.

the version of you I loved—
it's saved.

it makes me wonder—
do they understand love
in its truest form at all?
if they did,
they wouldn't say "just move on."

they'd say,
"I hope one day this love
will no longer be your haunting call."

- You Left, But I'm Still Here

I wake to the ache—
a hunger,
raw and endless,

for your skin,
your slow-motioned lips,
the scent of your perfume,
twisting like smoke around my ribs,
doing its quiet magic.

but why do I crave your eyes the most?

the way they split me open,
soft and devastating,
a place that stops time,
ripping through my fantasies.

a hypnosis transforming me—
woman to honey,
woman to animal,
wild in the most beautiful way.

a place I ache to drown.

lost in the moment,
I remember—
we aren't together anymore.

I betray my heart
each time I think of you.

what's the point
of craving love

that no longer exists
anywhere else
but in my body?

- My Body Still Thinks You're Mine

Let me tell you
why I'm jealous of the sun—

it gets to be
the light of your life,
the star of your whole day.

it's the reason
you get out of bed in the morning,
the one that sees your face
before anyone else.

it gets to stare at you,
anytime, every day.

it feels appreciated
as you soak in its attention.

it gets to make your heart race,
to kiss your skin
as much as it wants—
and you treasure the marks
it leaves behind.

it gets to see
the admiration in your eyes
as it falls asleep on the horizon.

it gets to make the world
feel like a brighter,
happier place.

it gets to bring

a smile to your face.
it gets to be your navigator
when you don't know the way.

it gets to see you
in your most vulnerable state,
when it's light and bright
and there's no darkness
to hide it away.

but most of all,
I'm jealous of the sun—

because it can't love you
like I do—

yet it still gets to be closer to you
than I ever can.

-Jealous of the Sun

How Do You Explain to Someone How Much They Hurt
You?

if I want to try,
my brain floats to so many emotions,
but they start bouncing off the wall,
and it's all too much
to put into one sentence
to describe it all.

and I'm left with one word: immense.

immensely sad,
immensely angry,
immensely lost
in feelings too dense.

how do you explain to someone
how much they hurt you,
without my jaw and shoulders
molding into a clench?

if only tears could speak—
can you imagine all the words
each tear would leak?

they'd explain
what I've been trying to explain to myself,
week after week.

how do you explain to someone
how much they hurt you?

my voice quivering
like paper flying through wind.

if the frequencies of my voice could speak,
can you imagine
all the painful noises they'd make?
the type of glass
they could break.

how do you explain to someone
how much they hurt you?

there are no words
that can explain.

if there were,
I wouldn't be in this much pain.

- How Do You Explain to Someone How Much They Hurt You?

I wanted you in this lifetime,
where we're both human,
completely engulfed in each other,
and life is painted only in happy colors.

but you are not mine today,
nor tomorrow,
and I'll never be able
to call myself your wife.

maybe in another life,
where we are trees,
or bees,
or birds—

or one where we can just love each other
and it doesn't hurt.

maybe centuries from now,
when life is lived on the moon.
I know it's not anytime soon,
but if I can't have you in this life,
I can't wait for this one
to be over and done.

so I can meet you again,
where mornings rise with another sun,
and you're beside me in bed.

where every hurtful word
we've ever spoken
has never even been said.

I can't wait for this life
to be over and done,

so I can call you my moon and stars again,
so I can call you my only one—
in the next lifetime to come.

-In Another Life

I tried,
but I can't save us.

everything I tried to create
vanished into thin air,
and now remains
particles of dust.

I've mixed so many potions,
to find the cure
to why you can't love me.

I lost hope
when I reached 333.

tell me why this is the end.

I spent days wishing,
praying for a sign—
a clue on which road to wend.

my arms melted
into elastic ribbons,
holding onto you
no matter where I went.

but you never held on to my hand,
never rushed to save me
as I sank into quicksand.

I've lost my grip,
staring into your loveless eyes.

so I wrote my goodbye in blood—
to remind you how
you let an innocent love die.

-The Last of Something Beautiful

My heart learned to beat for you—
every pulse in sync with your touch.

so when you left,
I asked for it back,
assuming its shape was still mine.

I tried to put it back into my chest,
but without your hands,
it just doesn't fit.

-*The Shape you Left me In*

If you'd let me,
I would love you so clearly—

yes, I said clearly.
I'd love you crystal clear,
and I wouldn't stop
for a million years.

I'd love you with the good and the bad.
I'd peel back all the layers of your skin,
get to see the damage
you never talk about,
but I know lives within.

I know you don't believe in any of this.
I can feel it in your eyes,
down to your lips.

but I'd love you just as much
as you don't believe in love.

if I knew you could let me in,
I'd come with a parade—
balloons, flowers,
the heavens,
and the whole sea.

I'd claim your heart,
and I'd never leave.

I'd show you what it's like
to be loved for free,
make you fall in love

with how much love you receive.

I'd make you believe
love was made just for the two of us.
I'd make myself the only person
you could finally say you trust.

but you're yellow without me,
and I'm blue without you.

what's the point
if I can only love you from a distance?
knowing you could forget me
in an instance?

I wonder—
if I stopped knocking,
would you finally open the door
and invite me in?

-Bruised Knuckles

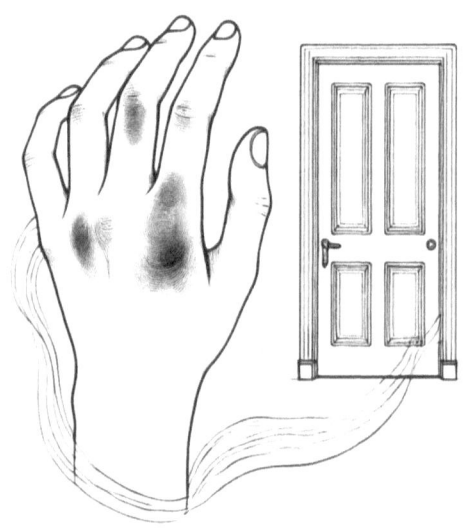

You looked for flaws.
you found some.
you liked some.
you welcomed some.

I wonder—
was that your way of finding reasons
to love me less,
and hate me more?

but then,
some got boring.
some weren't demanding,
weren't annoying.
some couldn't outshine the good things.

and that's when *some* wasn't enough—
not enough of a challenge to bring.

you crave flawless perfection,
but you need her flaws,
her daily rejections.

good
makes you want more of a mess,
toxic
keeps you wanting me, no less.

I've been her,
and her,
and her—
and all of the above.

what strange ways
you humans love.

-An Alien to your Love

I knew he was lying.

"It's just not the right time,"
"It's just not what I want right now,"
"It's just me and my commitment issues."

but it was never about time,
never about circumstance,
never about things moving too fast.

it was always about the right person.

and I wonder—

why wasn't I enough to be that person?
why wasn't my love,
overflowing and relentless,
the kind of love that could build worlds,
enough to make him stay?

I poured myself out in ways
no one else could.

in ways selfish hearts
couldn't even fathom—

sacrifices others wouldn't dare,
even to save a life.

my love was precious—
rare,
unshakable,
the kind of love you don't find twice.

but even gold is mistaken for a fake
by hands that don't know its worth.

and I guess sometimes,
a love too pure and real
is simply too heavy
for a counterfeit heart to stick around.

-More Than Greedy Hearts Can Carry

I can carry the weight
of the pain you gave me—

the love lost,
the future that crumbled,
the memories I'll force myself to forget,
the pieces of me you broke.

but time—

the time you stole,
the seconds,
the years—

I might find everything else I've lost,
but never the time
I gave to you.

-The Most Expensive Gift

59

Love has a fickle nature,
and I am no longer sure
the rain is worth a few rainbows,

no longer certain
the ache of thunder won't leave scars,
just for a fleeting arc of passion and color
that fades as quickly as it blooms.

love promises no happy endings,
only the certainty of the storm,
offering sunlight in fragments.

is it worth it to drown?
to tread water in the unknown,
never sure if you'll make it through
just to feel the shimmer
of light and love on your skin?

maybe love is the storm itself,
a beautiful chaos
that leaves you broken—
no matter how calm or furious
the sky seems tonight.

-*The Delicate Lie of Love*

I bit and chewed you up,
digested every trace—

only to realize
I have a stomach ache.

I swallowed you whole,
but now I can't remember
if you ever wanted me
to know how you taste.

-Bitter Remains

Belinda Daou

TRAUMA
IN
BROKEN SPACES

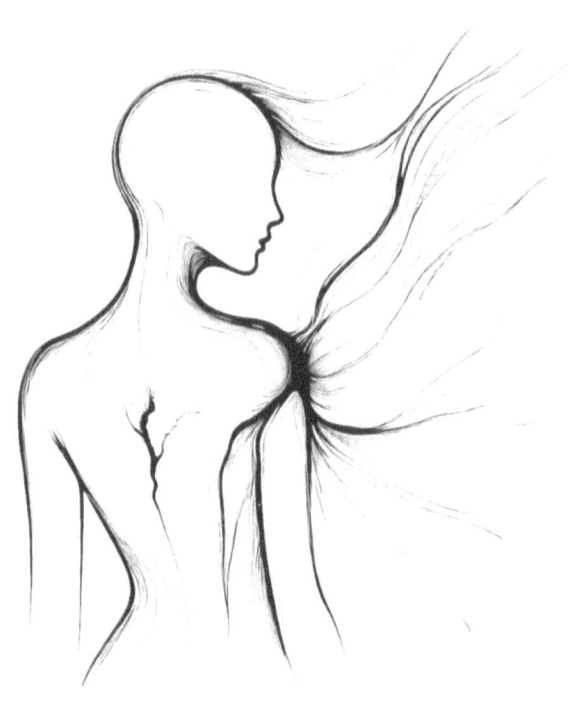

He was life,
and he was death—

and her soul
was sold to his heart.

a reckless deal,
in a moment of passion,
where love and ruin blurred,
and there was no turning back.

a fate sealed,
to contradicting arms,
wrapped in the chaos
of longing and loss.

-*The Cost of Him*

Fear feels like pain—

when what we fear
is a repetition
of what has already hurt us.

-*Déjà Vu*

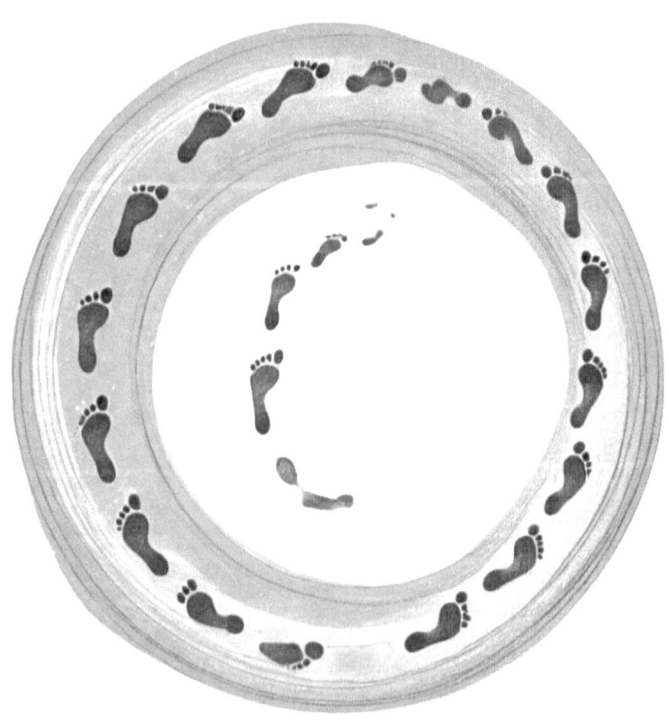

Falling in love—
what a toxic thing.

the eyes,
it always attacks the eyes.

it either turns them
into a flaw detector
or hypnotizes them
with a naïve-laced protector.

how can it be both,
so fiercely?

it either poisons you mad
or poisons you dumb.

both ways,
it's still poison.

-A toxic thing

Place your heart on the table,
bare, surrendered—

its rhythm a whisper
of everything you could never say,
everything you chose not to give.

leave.

carry with you the weight
of wounds you thought
would be mine alone.

go—
and never come back.

for some things,
once broken,
should never be returned—
nor forgiven.

-Now We Both have No Heart

Day by day,
I find myself falling out of love
with love—

not in a dramatic,
heart-wrenching way,
but in the quiet,

like the fading of sunlight
behind the clouds,

like petals loosening
their grip on the stem.

it's the slow unraveling of dreams
I once held tight,

the weight of words
that promised forever
but never quite fit
the shape of my soul.

love,
once a symphony,
now,
 a distant hum—
a song I've heard too many times
to still feel its meaning.

and yet, I wonder:

is it love I'm falling out of,
or the illusion

that it was ever going to last forever?

-I Am Done with Beautiful Lies

They say true love
is measured by the willingness
to die for someone.

well, I did—

not once,
but a hundred quiet deaths.

I died in every sacrifice,
in every piece of myself
I gave away.

in every silence
where my voice was buried
to let yours be heard.

I died over and over again—

until there was nothing left of me
but the shadow of your love.

leaving no space for life.
leaving no room to breathe.

-I Died So You Could Love Me

She didn't know
what love felt like anymore.

it came to her only in glimpses—
a shadow at the edge of a memory,
from another life,
from another girl.

like a song
she knew all the words to,
but sang jumbled,
inconsistent,
off-key.

she missed what it meant to be loved,
but forgot how it actually felt.

love became a language
she forgot how to speak,
another world—
ancestral, alien—
etched in a dialect
she'd never learn again.

a map she couldn't follow,
a place she knew existed,
but could never reach.

-Like Dust on An Old Map

I wore your words like a second skin,
didn't feel right,
but reshaping who I thought I'd been—

an ache I couldn't touch,
heavy as stones,
pressed down on my heart,
a reality I couldn't condone.

you planted seeds,
called them flowers,
said love was sharp,
it could bruise,
it could lose its patterns,
made it simple for you to lose your love,
your manners.

called me hard to handle,
hard to hold,
too easy to hate—
too easy to scold.

so I watered my weeds
till the water ran lifeless,
drowned my own voice
till it sank with my soul,

vines reaching deep into every breath,
every move,
every step—
a tangle I mistook
for learning to love you beyond depth.
each night,

I counted stars alone,
while you conjured clouds I couldn't see,
spun shadows into doubts I didn't need.

I shaped myself to reach you
without bleeding on your edges,
each look—
a needle, a knife,
a corner into wedges,
imprinting fear under my skin.

you called it care;
I learned to flinch,
every stare,
every footstep,
every inch.

to shrink—
from the sound of my own voice,
as if it might lead to chaos,
an unknown void,
a fate
I was blamed to choose.

I learned to cringe
at the sound of my own name,
lost ground,
lost air,
lost time and space—

a name fading in mirrors,
knowing neither face nor frame.
somewhere along the way,

I forgot what my energy felt like,
how my shine used to glow—
a stranger caught in your reality,
your show.

I wore myself thin,
erased line by line,
a faint beat
of what I was,
barely defined.

and after all the noise,
I sit,
peeling away
your fingerprints,
layer by layer,
breath by breath,

unlearning the sound of your voice inside mine,
finding the bones
you bent to breaking,
the fear you stitched
into my shaking,
the pieces you swore
were never there.

now when I step away,
I see—
there is still skin beneath these scars,
dried roots and muted music,
suppressed screams and tender bruises,

a pulse of someone I once knew—

a self lost,
trying to break through,
somewhere
between what's mine,
and what was you.

-Second Skin

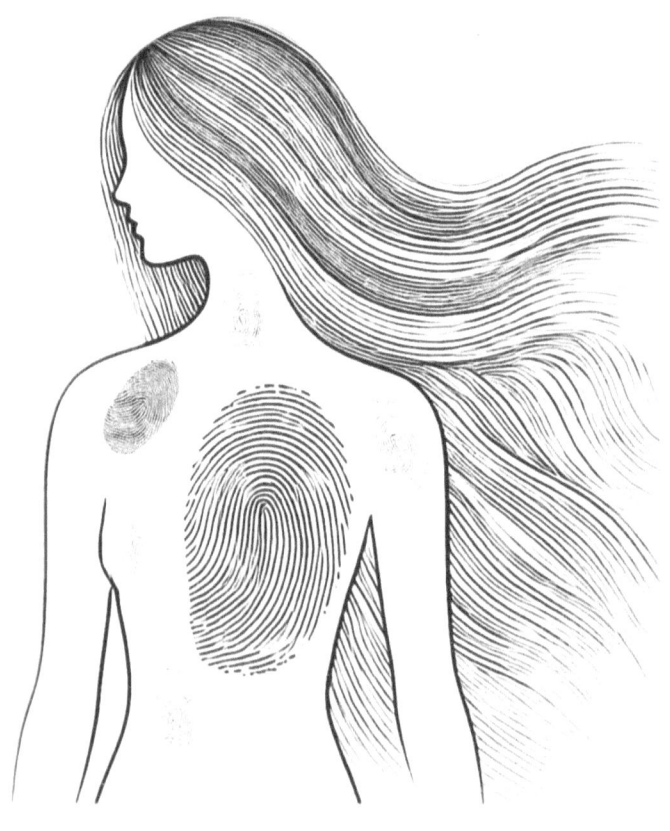

I tried to hold the flood,
bit my lip until it bled.

for you.
for me.
for the quiet part of me
that begged through the tears—

he's not worth the cry.

-Loving You Against My Will

I've always wanted to save
every man I've loved—

to patch the cracks,
smooth the edges,
make him whole.

but tonight, I wonder:

was I sculpting a savior
for my own reflection?
mending his flaws
to mask my own?
sewing safety nets
from broken strings,
so he wouldn't leave
before I let him go?

or was I holding
their shattered pieces,
hoping to heal
the little girl inside me—

the one who needed
someone to stay?

-Saviors I Tried to Build

You hurt me
in ways no bandage,
no resuscitation,
no cure can dominate.

I hope it makes you cry—
just a little,

enough for me to hand you
a fraction of my river.

-Just a Few Tears

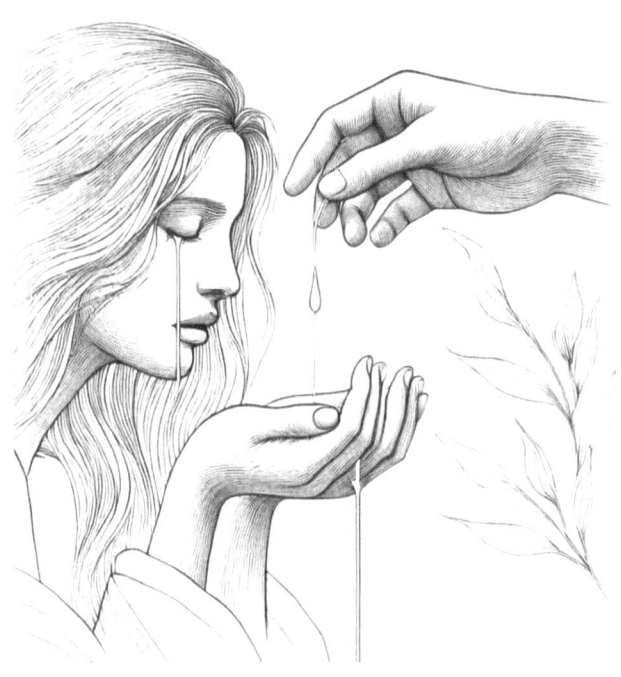

It wasn't your words
that gave up my heart,
it was your eyes
and the way they looked back.

the way you smiled
when you saw my face—
like you saw straight through me,
like you held my soul
in some eternal place.

now, when I sit with those moments,
I ask myself why?

why did it all feel so real?
how was I so wrong?
my heart caught up
in fairytale songs.

I was so sure it was you
the moment we met,
I saw magic,
I saw light—
memories I'll never forget.

I swore those eyes,
that smile,
were meant to stay,
etched in forever,
carved into my fate that day.

but maybe I was just
another fish in the sea.

I took the bait and dove deep,
thinking love was a promise meant to keep,
believing we were meant to be.

but when the truth hit—
the one I tried to ignore—
the way you looked at me with a hate
I'd never seen before,

it took over,
a poison that spread—
a darkness I never knew,
filled me with dread.

those eyes—
the ones that shattered
every truth I held close,
breaking the dream I loved most.

nightmares couldn't match
the pain they gave,
piercing so deep
I knew it was a love
I couldn't save.

how hard it is
to love someone so much
and have them deny its purity,
its touch.

when every fiber in me
belonged to your name,

yet my love was left
to bear the shame.

it's hard to see evil
in eyes you adored.

I prayed for light,
a heart restored,
questioned myself—
"how did I not see this before?"
hoped the eyes I loved
still lived at the core.

but the darkness kept me questioning—
how could love ever look like this?
how could something so sacred
deliver so much hate?

those eyes should have been my shelter,
not a place to break.

now, tell me—
how do I trust my heart again?

when you showed me that love—
was all just pretend?

-Ashes of A Dream

I know I have sad eyes.

Eyes that see beneath smiles,
beneath sweet words.
Eyes that trust no one—
not even the innocent—
but have seen too much to soften,
too much to shine,
too heavy to carry their own light.

They've cried heartbreaks
most wouldn't survive.
They've watched people leave
and left me seeing myself
through shattered mirrors.

They plant doubts—
in strangers I meet,
in friends I've known for years.
They're oceans of fears,
waves that could break a grown man,

the kind I try to bury,
but they always speak louder—
louder than love stories,
louder than tragedy,
louder than anything
I've ever dared to say.

I don't know why they're so sad,

but I think they broke

the day my sanity was blinded-
by all they've felt,
by all they've seen.

-*Broken World, Broken Eyes*

I never thought I'd hate love
as much as I do now.

who would've thought—

the thing you cherish most,
the thing you built your future around,
moved mountains for,

could bleed into your soul?

the thing that once felt like life itself
becoming your darkest pain,

the very thing
that could destroy you.

-*Love Was a Knife, and I Held It Tight*

You broke me—
not in the typical
broke-my-heart kind of way.

let me think—
how to put these words together to say:

you broke the part of me
that feels sparks on the first date,
the part that drives home smiling,
dreaming about what this could become one day.

you broke the part that stays up at night,
waiting for my phone to ring,
the part so smitten,
you could play me like a puppet on a string.

the part that cries at the slightest sting—
that part?
it's gone.

the tables have turned.
and now, every man is a pawn.

you broke the flirt in me,
the girth in me,
the rebirth in me.

a broken record played too many times—
it's lost its feeling.
it's lost its meaning.

a paralyzed heart,

like no buttons work to press restart.

I don't know if that makes my heart unique—
a work of art—
but it's lonely,
dying on me slowly.

hard as a rock.
I can't activate any feelings.
it's shut down, into locked,
shocked, and blocked.

no matter how hard I try to care,
there's really—
not much there.

you seem like a great guy,
but nothing about you
is going to give me that high.

I can't give you my heart,
but you can still go ahead
and try to apply.

-Paralyzed Heart

I know those eyes—

like the nightmare
I wake up screaming from,
clinging to the edges of my mind,
haunting even the brightest days.

they hold a story
I cannot unread,
a pain
I cannot unsee.

and still, I keep looking,
drawn to the darkness,
as if it might finally tell me
why I can't forget.

I know those eyes,
because they've followed me,
through every shadowed corner,
a silent reminder
of everything
I'm still trying to escape.

-I'll Never Forget His Eyes

They told me to be gentle,
to be soft,
to be more feminine.

they told me to hold my tongue,
to be more reserved,
to be more accepting,
to love with grace.

but these were the very things
that broke my heart,
again and again—

the lessons that taught me
how to shatter quietly,
how to bleed without a sound.

they told me to be everything
that made it easier
for the world to hurt me.

but they never told me
how to survive myself.

-Crowned in Fragility

We are tiptoeing around clarity,
on a merry-go-round
that won't slow down.

neither in one place nor another—
just grey.

grey was the theme color,
where nothing was ever quite clear.
because that's how he wanted it to be.

he didn't want to slow down—
that's where his cunning mind
might finally be revealed.

as long as we stayed
on this blurry whirlwind ride,
he could push the truth to the side,
claiming it was all just how
I chose to perceive it in my mind.

what he's done—

I couldn't call it wrong or right,
just another personal excuse.

where does the line begin or end
when we talk about emotional abuse?

but now, I see you.

right there,
tiptoeing,

behind you too,
observing you—

not the way you want
to be perceived anymore.

now,
I choose—
let's say—
through love-dying eyes,
and a view
closer to the truth.

-The Gray of Emotional Abuse

I never was one
to fall in love easily.

I never was one
to be loved back easily either.

and maybe that's why,
when I'm in love,
I feel like the biggest fool.

it was so hard for you
to let me love you.

I don't know why
I didn't give up sooner.

actually, I do.

I've always been
a warrior for love—
giving up was too painful.

how could I abandon
what makes me who I am?

I saw your darkness,
and still admired
every light at the end of your tunnel.

I let my memory
wash out your flaws,
like dipping a black paintbrush in water,
hoping the color would fade.

I made sure
your brightest colors
dominated the walls
of my long-term memory.

I praised them,
watered them into a long life,
kept them bright and shiny.

I moved parts of myself aside—
parts I wanted to keep—
just to make room
for you to want to stay,
to give you a space inside me
you could call home.

I made my body a healing pod,
a place for you to lay
when the inside of your soul
needed to be hugged.

it didn't matter
if I was blinking,
screaming "battery low."

not everyone can do that.

what does that say about you?
what does that say about me?

I think it makes me
far stronger than you could ever be.
I gave you so much,

and you couldn't even love me.

be careful who you call weak.

I am not weak
for loving a man
who couldn't love me back.

to go in heart-first,
knowing you might not come out alive—

that isn't weakness.

that is bravery
wrapped around
a selfless, loving heart.

but you—

your heart is sitting
on the sidelines,
afraid of all the love
pouring out of mine.

-I Was the Only Soldier

There's so much of the past
and so little of the future.

telling me to focus
on what doesn't exist
is asking me to build
a bridge over nothing,

to forget the scars
I wear like tattoos—
sketched reminders
of every battle I survived.

the future is a faint,
uncertain whisper,

but the past
screams in my face,
and I hear it
every day.

-Positivity Defect

"Crazy Lazy

Don't take it personal, baby.

You want me to love you?

Just do what I tell you to."

*But what if he
leaves me— out of
the blue?*

"Delusional. Psycho.

My bad—

didn't mean to send that message,

it was just a typo."

*Could this be the
reason he walks
away, though?*

"Emotional. Sensitive.

Let me give you love as a sedative.

Your feelings right now aren't even relative."

Silent treatment for days and days...

I just hope he loves
me enough to stay.
What now?

Does this mean we
broke up?

I didn't listen.

He told me

he was fed up.

"Cry baby—

morning and night,

streams and lakes.

Look at your face,

And how your hands shake."

I'm a mess.

If I'm such a
headache,

do I even
deserve love in
the first place?

Self-worth crumbles

with every game he plays.

his eyes tell me I'm a burden in every way.

"I told you, that's what you heard—
It's not what I meant to say."

"Monster. Disturbed creature.
I need love,
not a mom or a teacher.
I don't want to talk about your feelings either."

What have I
done?

Am I really that
evil?

It's a nightmare,

yet I'm wide awake.

My mind is yours-

wired,

Into a level 10 earthquake

"Lousy.

Worthless.

Piece of shit.

Ten personalities,

and they're all split.

Manipulative.

Mental.

Toxic.

Stay away from her—

run away real quick."

*Is that what he's
telling
everyone?*

*Am I really
twisted and
sick?*

I believed you for years—

And somewhere deep down,

I still do.

You dismantled my brain

until I believed it was true.

97

And that stays with me—

Every time

I meet someone new.

-Gaslighter

My jaw clenches on my anxiety,
my shoulders rise in defense.

my teeth grind
beneath the weight of anger,
my arms tremble under fear.

my fingers stiffen,
locked in doubt.
my voice—
loud and muted
all at once.

this is what you do to my body
every time you unleash your abuse.

you turn me into a battleground,
a war I cannot refuse.

-I Hold Your Violence in My Bones

Don't look too deep into my eyes.
don't listen too closely to my voice.
don't read between the words I say.
don't search for the truth I'm trying to hide.

because I'm fighting every piece of me,
every trembling part,
just to keep you from knowing
how much I love you.

I want my eyes to lie,
to blind you with deceiving brilliance.

because the moment you see my love,
your monster wakes,
and I drown in the fear
of you walking away.

-Your Weapon of Choice: My Heart

I don't know why I miss you sometimes.

you showed me hell on earth,
and still,
I miss you.

you dragged me
into the darkest corners of myself,
sank your teeth
into the softest parts of my soul,
birthing ugliness
I can't unsee.

you devoured
what was gentle in me,
leaving scars
where trust once lived.

and yet,
I still miss you.

not the real you.

I miss the man
who made me fall in love,
the man who might never have existed.

maybe he was a figment of your betrayal,
a masterpiece of my imagination,
a projection of the man
I desperately wanted you to be.

whoever he was,

I loved him.

badly. entirely.

even if he was a lie.

so when I say I miss him,
nobody needs to understand.

it's enough that I carry
longing and shame
in the same heart.

-The Delusion of Us

You taught me love—

with hands that bruised,
words that cut,
and a smile that lied.

now,
I flinch at kindness,
question warmth,
and mistake love for pain.

-Love, or Something Like It

I threw my heart into your hands,
thinking you'd hold it tight
and pour your soul into it.

that you'd catch it so quickly,
hold it so close to your body,
take it on an adventure—
filled with banging drums
and "I found the love of my life" anthems.

until I realized—

you caught it with bent fingers.

indifferent fingers,
clumsy, indecisive fingers,
fingers with no direction.

you caught it,
but fumbled with it,
dragged it around like a burden.

a burden so heavy in your hands.

forgetting where you left it at times,
nails scratching all the sensitive parts,
dropping it here and there—
it became old wear and tear.

you choked out every heartbeat
it used to make when it saw your face.

you gave it back to me

in its worst condition—

bruised, scratched, drained,
barely beating.

I don't want it back.

I have nothing left in me to fix it,
only to have it die
on someone else's table again.

-Bent Fingers

Soft as a baby's blanket,
tender as a fresh wound.

fragile bones,
and eyes that flinch
beneath the glare
of a cruel world.

a heart so empathetic,
it bled for everyone—
until it drained itself dry.

once warm,
once whole,
now cold as a mountain's peak.

eyes dulled to the color of sorrow,
a brutal past
carving trenches in her soul.

is this what it means
to love too much?

for the world to take a good heart,
crush it beneath its weight,

and twist it with pain—
until it becomes something darker,
something it was never meant to be

-*The Cold Got to Me*

It doesn't matter
how beautiful your skin is,
how strong and protective
your arms once felt,
how deadly handsome you look
when the sun paints halos on your face,
and your eyes burn into me
like promises I know
you'll never keep.

it doesn't matter—

not your angelic glow,
not your charming smile,
not your fairytale words,
not the endless "I'm sorry, it won't happen again,"
a lie that cuts deeper
than the bruises ever could.

because your beauty is a blade,
sharpened on my softness,
and now your arms
are what I fear the most.

your strength leaves me trembling,

and your pretty face—
the one I once believed
could never hurt me—
has turned into a curse.

you twisted everything beautiful about you,
and the very things I once adored

are now transformed
into red flags
I can't help but fear.

they say you invite
what you are used to.

he's used to chaos,
used to abandonment—
but so am I.

how can I fear it,
how can I run from it,
when I've lived surrounded by it
for so long?

and yet,
he calls it home,
while I tremble at its door.

he makes me cry
and feels nothing,
his eyes gleaming
as if my pain is his masterpiece,
as if the cracks in me
are his triumph.

as if he can only measure love
by the depth of my suffering.

why do I love beyond my scars,
while he carves into me
every wound he's ever carried?

why do I bleed for a love
that knows only how to destroy,
a love
that wears chaos like a crown
and calls its ruin
devotion?

-King of Childhood Trauma

Most people get hurt—
they get stitches
wrap it tight
bandage it up
let it breathe
let it heal

but me

I just keep bleeding

- *No Stitches for This*

You traced my cracks
with steady hands
memorized the fault lines
where I'd bleed most

every weakness
you learned by heart

to make sure
your blade
became my scar

-Artfully Scarred Intentions

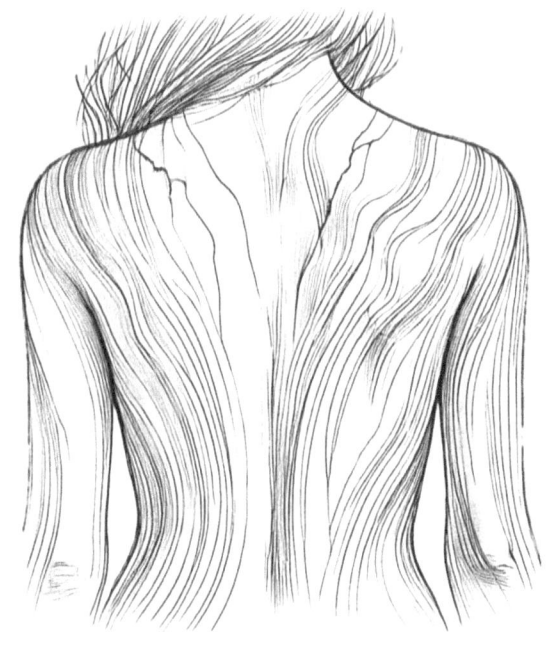

I'd set myself on fire
just to keep you warm

I don't have a name for that kind of love
only the assumption
that you made me this way

built to break
designed to take
more than you'd ever give

maybe it was always the plan—
to strip me bare
to empty myself out
to love myself less

so I'd have all this love leftover
to give away

-Silent Hypnosis

I created illusions
of what we could be
tried to rewrite our story
to fit my dreams

I wrote on empty pages
in permanent ink
but you tore them apart
before the words could sink

only to discover
all along

you had written the ending
before we even met

-Hidden Ink

It's hard to describe it—
let me try.

Have you ever felt so sad,
you knew it was going to last forever?

Even though you don't know,
it just feels like it.

Because there's so much of it,
it seems impossible for it to leave you.

When did I get here?

It makes you think—
how far you can travel in such little time,
how long you can stay in just one place.

Time keeps moving,
while I take a nap
in this tight, heavy space.

-*Untranslatable Paralysis*

I'm going to eat my words,
so you don't choke on the truth—

swallowing silence
was always easier for you.

-Why Do I Always Have to Lie to You?

I go through my phone,
scavenging pictures of us.

Maybe I'm trying to piece you together,
to lose myself in the photographs,
to blur the edges of reality—

where you were the man I loved,
and not the monster
you truly are.

-The Man in the Pictures

You think you only broke my heart—
six months of missing,
of longing,
of sewing jagged edges back together.

a classic heartbreak story.

but you took much more than that.

you stole my innocence,
scratched trust into unrecognizable shapes,
a navigator lost in trauma's fog.

trusting wholly is foreign now.
so foreign I can't even trust
what's inside my own skin—
a language my body unlearned.

I sleep with my eyes open,
walk with my shoulders shuddering,
speak in a flinch, in defense—
fluent in hypervigilance.

you turned my mirrors into liars,
my mornings into storm clouds.

the sun doesn't shine where I live.

you painted halos black
on strangers I haven't met yet.

I see demons where there were once faces,
hear deceit laced in words meant to be soft.

you plucked faith from the edges of my soul,
the parts that still wanted to believe in good things.

you rewrote every fairytale,
penned in the ink of abuse and betrayal.

you didn't just break me—

you rewrote the world.

-My Narcissist

You didn't love me—
you conditioned me

fed me just enough warmth
to keep me from the cold
before hitting me with ice

just enough kindness
to keep me from leaving
before your rage took over

just enough pain
to keep me craving more
before your torment blurred into delusion

just enough kisses
to make my skin miss your lips
before those same lips
slashed at my self-worth

just enough promises
to keep me dreaming of a future
before you crumbled my world to bits

chaos became passion
conflict became connection

your apologies—
a serenade of love

you changed me
then told me I made you toxic

you broke me
then told me I needed you to heal

I let you rewire my mind
hooked on the high of your approval
the barely-lit spark in your eyes
the crash of your absence
the panic in your threats to leave

the cycle of hurt and comfort
that felt too much like love

you made me an addict to your chaos
to the way your lips and hips found mine
while my tears were still falling

a fool for believing
love was something I had to suffer for

I learned to live with your poison
but you convinced me
your love was the only cure

I learned to crave the lows
so I could feel the highest of the highs

and each time I try to withdraw
suddenly nothing else matters—
but your flakes of love

I search for you
like your scent is my only high
the only thing I want to live for

and I wonder—
how many times
I will have to relapse
before I can look at you
before I can tell my arms
not to reach for you again

-Trauma Bonded

I know I've earned some forgiveness from God
for every time I forgave your devilish games
for every time I loved you
while you treated me like nothing

for every mistake you made
that I tried to hide from the world
for every sorry I accepted
that you never meant
for every apology I gave
in the name of empathy
in the name of peace

for every sacrifice I made
to keep you happy
to keep you from baring your teeth
for every lie you told
that I wanted so desperately to believe

for every bruise
I convinced myself to forgive

for every childhood trauma
I used to justify your rage

for every prayer I whispered for you
that you never cared for

for every time you called me the devil
an animal a monster
for every *may God punish you*
you screamed in my face like a curse—

God knows
God sees

He knows you
and He knows me

now I wonder
how this monster you've named
can still get down on her knees
and still pray for you
still feel bad for you

because I can only imagine
the endless depths of forgiveness
you'll need

-*The Paradox of Loving Monsters*

The fear in my eyes
was your drug
your fix

your demons smirked
right through your face
your inner child's cry
for control
for attention

you got high
on the desperate cracks
of my voice
the vibrations of my body
shaking itself
into a mess

the tears I couldn't stop
even if I tried—
begging
desperate

and while you feasted
on my breaking
on my screaming
on my panic attack
on the bathroom floor

I prayed
like I'd never prayed before—

for God to take me
anywhere
but here

in any way
by any means

-The Hell You Built for Me

SELF REFLECTING
IN
BROKEN SPACES

When your eyes begin to flutter slow
weighed down by the energy drained into your tears
and you're finally exhausted enough
to let your face relax to un-crumple—

in that moment the world has already ended
a massive explosion
shattering through the cracks of your heart

words sit heavy in your throat
but they're lost in the shock
the only sound that escapes
are confused mumbles

as your lashes close over the wet puddles
resting under your eyes
your focus narrows
to your heavy-hearted sighs

this heartbreak didn't knock softly
it came banging at your door in the night
and you know
come morning its echoes
will only grow louder

you convince yourself
the pain you fell asleep with
is just for tonight
that by tomorrow
it won't taste as sour
but morning comes
your phone is dry of love
no apology

no text messages

and your body feels like it's aged ten years overnight
your eyes open
and the thoughts of last night
crawl back to you one by one
like lightbulbs flickering on in a dark room

the memory of every thought
that made you cry consumes you again
like grey clouds smothering
a once-promising blue sky

and the rain in your eyes begins to shake
you've never been more aware
of the ache inside your chest

pain fills the room
settling in like it belongs here
like it's not just passing through—
but here to stay

last night wasn't a nightmare
this is real
they're really gone

somewhere elsewhere
and you're left behind
abandoned, disoriented—
stranded in the middle of nowhere and everywhere

-Between Yesterday and Tomorrow

My color is blue
I didn't have a clue
I was made up of such a happy and sad color—
that I could be a father a mother a lover
but also layers of another yet to uncover

all those heaven-and-hell shades of blue

some days I'll be the bright cheerful one that makes your
day
following the sun spreading light over the grey
all those innocent and insidious shades of blue

some days the deep cold dark ones come out to play—
the ones that will make you say
how much darkness do I need to crawl out of to finally
get away

as much as you hate me
you know I'm fascinating

baby blue powder electric
crystal sapphire arctic
royal steel teal

you love every shade of how I feel

-*The Shades of Blue I Carry*

My heart has legs now

as long as it's moving
it can't sit still
to create a mind of its own

as long as it's moving
it can't be caught
nor stolen away

as long as it's moving
it sure as hell can't fall
into anyone's back pocket again

-Too Fast to Catch

I'm always the nice one
the pleaser
the sweet one
the good girl—
always been too empathetic
to be the teaser

the one with trust issues
the past the damage
yet somehow
the relationship appeaser

the understanding one
the mental health professional
listens and listens
but always ends up the confessional

names I hate
labels I want to keep under the table
how can I just reset disable
instead superglue words on me like rough
but can't get enough

"can't tell if she'll break my heart
or if it's all a bluff"
"gives love but walks away
as soon as it gets tough"

the taker before the giver
the self-lover first
heart of steel—beautiful
but the absolute worst
the heartbreaker routine rehearsed

I want to be her
I want to be her
I want to be her

toughen up this stupid heart
rearrange my priorities
subtract sweet
until I equal just smart
reset my emotions lure you in
even with big fat warning signs
scribble out the sweet kind
redefine my character lines

I don't want to be me anymore
I want to be bad
I want to be a beauty and a beast
devouring you right here on this floor

I'm the owner of a messy heart—
bent and broken with the weakest roar
sacrificed my own heart to keep yours
the giver
never the receiver

who taught me to be such a fucking fairytale believer
who told me to always be so emotionally clever

put all the weight on my shoulders
while you walked away—a feather

I'm sick of being the victim in every story
as if that's how it ends
like it's mandatory

fuck all of that
it always ends with my heart
being stomped on flat

I want to be the one holding the sword
piercing through your chest—
blood dripping from your heart
and yet you still think you're blessed

for once I want to be her—
the bad guy the wild one
the one who got away completely un-stressed
the one you'll never forget
the one who left you
completely obsessed

-It's My Turn

Find me and love me
not in passing
not in pieces
but fully deeply

like it's new to my body
like it's the first time love
ever dared to touch me

find me and love me
before bitterness has its way with me
before time eats at the hope
I held onto for so long

find me and love me
before I forget how to love
before I forget
I ever even wanted to

-Bitter Woman to Be

You can have my heart—
but only if you can color it again

fill the cracks with shades I've forgotten
paint over the stains I've bled into it

turn ruin into art

if you cannot make me glow
leave me in the dark

if you can't make me whole
leave me cut in half

love it bold
or leave it blank

-Paint Me Happy or Leave Me in My Misery

Her heart was bigger than the whole goddamn world—

it overflowed with love
but love so vast it couldn't be seen for its beauty
misunderstood as a curse instead

too raw too untamed
to fit neatly into anyone else's small chests

they didn't know how to comprehend
a love so big—

it poured out like rivers
unstoppable and free
but the hands that tried to hold it
were always too weak—

always trembling under its weight

they wanted her in fragments manageable pieces—
as if something infinite
could ever be trimmed down
to fit their shallow timid hearts

her love was too big to satisfy—
a hunger no one dared to meet

she gave and gave
until she was empty—
until her heart grew hollow—

an aching void of potential
a paralysis of the soul

that still longed to give—

echoing with prayers
for people who only ever worshiped themselves

and so she learned to carry her heart alone—
to cradle its immensity in her own arms

she poured her love into men in fairytale books
and the stories they spun in her dreams—

the only ones
who wouldn't run from its flood

her heart was bigger than the whole goddamn world

and maybe that's why
its fate was to echo inside its own big hollow walls—
a sanctuary of love
too big for anyone else to inhabit

-*A Heart Too Big for a World Too Small*

All the love I've lost
to hearts with no return address—
who clears the debt?

do I bill the moon
for the sleepless nights?
the gods
for the fine print in their plans?
or the mirror
for smiling like it knew better?

-The Debt is Mine

She craved an old-fashioned kind of love
one far from where she existed today

her heart couldn't bear to settle
for shallow love

she wanted the real thing
even if it meant traveling through galaxies
and dimensions to find it

she longed for the kind of love
that poets wrote about
the kind that lingers in the air

where a single glance
could light up the darkest room
and every moment felt rare

she knew what she wanted
and if she couldn't have it
she didn't want anything at all

she dreamed of a love that felt like home
one that would hold her through life's storms
and still remain

a love so powerful
it would break the chains of time

a bond so unshakable
it would only grow with age

to her love wasn't just a passing desire

it was a fire that needed to burn bright

she refused to settle
for anything less than extraordinary

for she knew her heart's worth
knew what felt right

and so she wandered—
heart open but never desperate

waiting for the one
who'd meet her in the stars

because if love wasn't timeless
if it didn't consume her soul

she'd rather stand alone in her own light
than dim herself for anything less than whole

-The Kind of Love Poets Wrote About

It's never who
it's how—

the depth of your hands
when they hold
the weight of your words
when they fall
the warmth you leave
in the space between breaths

the heart doesn't ask
for labels
it asks for impact—

for the way love
feels like light
or fire
or both

-A Place Without Names

I don't wish to be unbroken
or to take back all the years that were stolen
I don't wish for nights without tears
or mornings where I could rise
without the weight of my fears

I don't wish there was someone who held my hand
protecting me from red flags
and warning signs I couldn't understand
I don't wish to un-love eyes
that hid goodbyes beneath their lies

I don't wish for a life of happy faces
if it means I'd never learn to smile
through the darkest spaces
I don't wish back days of innocence and light
if I don't know what darkness feels like—
to appreciate the warmth
when the sun comes back shining bright

because that person
the one who's never felt life's ugliness
its poisonous sting
wouldn't know what to do
with the pain living brings

they wouldn't know
how to welcome their feelings in
but run away from everything
they wouldn't know
what it's like to love unconditionally
to discover how big their heart is—
and how big it can grow

the capacity of love they have to give

they wouldn't understand
what it means to sacrifice
every ounce of time and energy
to someone who doesn't deserve it—
and still find peace to forgive

they wouldn't know the difference
between genuine love
and the love they had to beg for
again and again
they wouldn't know what it feels like
to hope and be patient

to hope and be patient and pray—
when God when

they wouldn't know what it feels like
to have their heart ripped out of their chest
and then to piece it back together—
like a thousand-piece puzzle
where nothing seems to quite fit

they wouldn't know what it's like
to stand on the edge
so close to losing their soul
their will to live—
and still dig deep deep down
to find the strength
not to give up and quit

I don't wish to be unbroken

each and every shattered piece was a lesson—
a part of the person I am today

the person who earned their power
through scars through shattered pieces
through the blackest days

the person who lives each day
holding the wisdom to now know—

where hope should bloom
and when to let go of anything
that doesn't want to stay

-Unbroken

I refuse to be
a trophy on your shelf of lies
polished by your fake glory
a prop in your deception game

I'm not your win
not your prize—
I'm the flame you couldn't put out
the fire burning through your disguise

-I Want to Be the Anxiety That Breaks You

All we can do is hope—

that the darkness in our souls
eventually cracks
letting in just enough light
to lead us toward more peaceful days

that sadness in silver drops
soaks the roots of something new
nourishing gardens of quiet smiles
until joy spreads like wildfire

that anger unravels
thread by thread
carried off by healing winds
making the weight of our past
easier to shed

that the blackened parts of us
aren't curses—

but constellations
waiting to align
waiting to make sense of it all

waiting for the light
to show us the pieces
we forgot were ours

-Prayers In the Dark

Pain leaves fingerprints on the soul
a weight that changes you
reshapes the way I see the world
how I breathe
how I love
how I trust

it rewires the heart
makes it beat differently—
sometimes slower
sometimes too fast

takes you to places your mind can't even perceive
fades out old dreams
that no longer make sense
with the way your heart beats

I mourned the pieces I lost
the softness
the innocence
the easy laughter
the lightness that once lit me

but in that grieving
I learned to listen to those pieces
I learned to rebirth them differently
to let them find new life in the cracks

because the heart though it cracks
learns to hold space
for both pain and healing
for both ache and joy
for both tears and smiles

to bend without breaking

and the mind though tangled by fear
learns to hold space
for both hope and worry
for both light and darkness
for both peace and chaos—
to grieve without suffering

so I gathered what remained
not to rebuild who I was
but to honor who I've become—

a mosaic of brokenness and resilience
each wound an opening to wisdom
a reminder that I survived

and though life carved scars into my story
scars that time cannot undo
I decide who I am going to be next

I choose to be more than my fragments—
stronger in my softness
happier in my sadness
and whole enough in my becoming

a work of art
that makes you smile and cry at the same time
crafted from all that was broken

-Mosaic

There's this little voice in me
static in the background
buried beneath all the hurtful noise
whispering *keep going*

even when every part of me
is screaming
you're too broken for redemption

but static is still sound

and for now
I'll cling to it
like a lifeline

-*The Only Sound That Matters*

I'm scared to live too fast
I'm scared to live too slow
how do you know
if the road you're on
is the right one to go

I'm scared to care too much
about the small things
that are just for show
and care too little
for the things
that will actually help me grow

I'm scared
to love the wrong people
and ignore the ones
who could be keepers
I'm scared to be too much of me
too slow
and too little of me
too fast

I'm scared
I could be just one decision away
from a whole different life
yet too weak
to ever take my own advice

I'm scared of living too young
for too long
forgetting
that I've always been an old soul

but I'm also scared of cutting my youth short
just because
time says
I need to grow old

-The Time Between Maybe

I hate that I hate my life
I hate the weight I carry
unseen

I hate my heart
for feeling small
for breaking
when there's no one to call

I hate my heart
for breaking so loud
for feeling lost
within a crowd

I hate the smiles that others wear
while I'm drowning
gasping air

I hate the silence
hate the noise
hate the emptiness
that steals my voice

I hate the crowd
how I disappear
a ghost
when anyone draws near

I hate the mirror
its empty stare
the frowning face
that's always there

I hate this anger I fight inside
I hate the time
I let slip by

I hate that I still can't find a clock that works
to make up for every wasted hurt

I hate everything—
and yet I stay
hoping hate
will hate me someday

-The Cracks That Hold Me

Belinda Daou

The hardest prison to leave
is not made of stone nor steel

it's the walls I built with trembling hands
a fortress meant to shield and heal

built to keep out friends and demons
protection from what could invade
steal and betray—
but freedom invites in
beautiful things bound to fade

each brick was laid to guard my heart

each click of a lock a vow
never let anyone close enough to hurt me
yet the chains of comfort
turned into a lifeless cage somehow

too far from the world
to remember how to feel
too far from life
to know what's real

the hardest prison is not outside—
it's the fear within
where I choose to hide

-I Never Meant to Live Here

How do I keep my soul
in a world colored in black and grey
how do I protect my aura
and let all the dark colors wash away

I've lost touch with the part of me
that believes in good people—
they all lied when they said they wouldn't hurt me
when they said they'd stay

I've lost faith in believing good prevails
that the devil always ends up slayed

how many times have I sat by the window
watching the good things in my life walk away

God tell me how I should talk to You
tell me how I should pray

the tighter I grip the faster they die
the deeper the hurt
the harder it is to open my eyes
tired of witnessing happiness all around me
when it seems allergic to my skin

they say believe stay positive keep up your chin
I have I've been

I've kept my head raised to the sky for years on end
but my neck is tired of looking up
at what's not mine at what could have been

you look at me and see tired and depressed

but you don't know the inner work I had to sustain

call me someone who uses my emotions more than my
brain
but my thoughts are invested in giving my heart pain

positivity creates change
great

if only you could see my invisible chains
one of the hardest things to explain
yet my eyes—still fixated on the goals
climbing
and still climbing
and still climbing

but I can't see the finish line at the end of the lane
feels like I'm climbing straight into insane

does anyone feel my pain
because it feels lonely standing on this side of the train

destination unknown
fighting for the unknown

I just need God to tell me I'm not alone
because if this is what it takes to smile again
I'm not sure I'll make it to the throne

-Praying for Just a Few Smiles

I put myself back together
in the strangest ways—

with threads pulled from panic attacks
needles forged from bitter truths
pins jabbed into what little self-love I had left
and fragile patches stitched from borrowed hope

in whatever way I could
I pieced myself together—

just enough to wake up
just enough to stand again

-What's Left of Self-Love

I searched for homes
in other people's hearts
for happiness
in their shallow eyes
for acceptance
in fragile words
they didn't even mean

I looked through their windows
hoping to see myself reflected
chased their attention
to feel self-respect
craved their love and approval
like it was the air
I couldn't breathe without

I was so desperate to be loved
I forgot how to love myself

I poured out everything I had
but left nothing for me
I didn't matter without them—
almost as if my existence
was insignificant without witnesses

peace was never in their hands
love was never in their eyes
home was never in their arms

it was here all along—
buried in my mind
beating in my chest
waiting in the silence of my soul

I just had to stop running
and learn how to come home

-Learning How to Get Home

Tattooed on my skin
in time this too shall pass—
a promise I wear
a prayer I whisper
when the weight feels unbearable

I trace the letters
again and again
as if my touch could wake the words to life
as if belief alone
could make the pain move faster

but time lingers
the pain stays
and I'm still here—
looking staring praying
waiting for the promise
to pass too

-The Promise That Won't Pass

If I could only hope less
I'd spread wings into unknown territory—
like a moth drawn to flames I know will burn
fly to ideas I already know I'd regret
run off the edges I've feared—
the risks I let die as dreams undone
buried beneath the rubble of hesitation

I'd love recklessly
let go of being the best version for him
just to see what gives—
feel the thrill
of chaos
the rush
of uncertainty

I'd find freedom in the absence
of regret and expectation—
the constant hum of anxiety
buzzing in my ear
like a hive swarming inside my skull
always wondering
where each decision might lead

imagine—
no weight of what could be
no chains of what should be
only the stillness
of an unwritten future

without hope
maybe the sky would open wider
stars falling

without the burden of wishes
I'd freefall into fate's hands
let go of the illusion of control
and finally learn—

that whatever is meant to be
would simply...
be

-Where Peace Lives

I know you've been through hell
but that means we have secrets to unpack
truths to unearth
and wounds we can't keep ignoring

you don't have to hide
I'm not the rest of the world
I'm not the noise outside these walls

if anyone deserves to see your scars
it's me
I've seen the worst of you
felt every ache in your body
carried the weight
and I'm still here
I've always been here

and even if the numbness takes over
even when it feels like you can't love yourself
I'll always remind you
that I do

-Let Me Help You Heal Us

I'm more trouble
than anything beautiful enough to keep—
at least that's what they tell me

in sighs
too heavy
in eyes
losing hope
in footsteps
walking away
in doors
that never open again

I take up space like a storm cloud
Heavy
looming
unwelcome
I speak and the air thickens
I stay and the room empties
I love and I hear hearts break

they patch me up with patience
but I tear right through it
they hold me close
then let me go—
like fire
too wild to keep

maybe I was made this way—
too much
too restless
too sharp at the edges
too hard to hold without bleeding

maybe they're right
maybe
I am more trouble than I'm worth

but trouble
shakes the ground
trouble
sparks the change
trouble
refuses to be silenced
to shrink
to fade

and if I am trouble
then let me be a storm
let me be wildfire
let me be both
a cure and a disease
let me be a beautiful kind of chaos

let me be the kind of trouble
they wish
they had learned to love

-I Am Beautiful Too

My heart shakes
at the thought
of letting someone in

I think I finally understand
the damage it left behind

it feels forgettable
irrelevant
when my armor is buckled tight
and no one is knocking at the door

but when a thud hits that hard exterior
despite its flattery
it feels more haunting than inviting

and my heart breaks
with every buckle I pull
every strap I tug at
trying to undo
what once kept me safe

I never imagined vulnerability
could feel like this—
not a release not a relief
but the slow ache
of reopening a wound
that took forever to heal

-I Don't Want to Bleed Again

Time and time again
drops trace my skin
rocky roads stained down my cheeks

pat them dry—
I refuse to cry

drops on my tongue
tastes of salt
salted all those words I swallowed
burning bitter

bit my tongue instead
bled out every letter unspoken
every ache unsaid

drops in my eyes
the sting of nights I soaked in my own grief

blink squint
digest them into goodbyes

I am ready—
to drain sorrowed water clinging to me
to wash away
the tears still drowning inside.

-*What Water Remembers*

I sit with the silence
its weight heavier than the screams
that burned through my throat

this quiet isn't peace—
it's the absence of chaos
chaos that has always felt like home

I touch my scars
some carved into my skin like brutal reminders
others buried deep where no one can see—
each one a map of battles fought and lost

I trace their edges when they burn for attention
and I wonder how I survived
when so much of me didn't

I know myself
and yet I don't

after all this breaking
it's like staring at a stranger—
a stranger I both fear
and long to hold
like a child of my own

I'm not whole
I don't think I ever will be
but I've found shards of myself
sharp stubborn pieces
I refuse to abandon

I'll force them back together

even when they slice my hands open
even when it hurts to hold myself

I'll put myself back together again—
brick by brick
scar by scar
with damaged hands
that shake
that bleed

but will never let go

and though I'll never forget
all that I've lost
I wear the proof
that I'm still here

the cracks in me don't just let the light in
they scream at the world
that I have survived the dark

-The Shapes I've Built Through Survival

There's a space
between surviving something
and truly feeling hope again

I am here
in the quiet aftermath—
where the world keeps moving
but I stand still

a silence that isn't peace
a pause that isn't rest—
a moment where I am still
trying to catch my breath

right now
I am lost in that distance
where survival whispers
isn't this enough?
but hope is too far away
to answer

-Between Breaths

In the quiet
between
what was and what remains
I learned to exist

to hold the weight
of shattered moments
to breathe
where it hurt the most

to search for myself
in left over pieces
in spaces I thought
would remain empty

because even in broken spaces
I learned to breathe again

-Breathing in Broken Spaces

About the Author

Belinda Daou has been writing since childhood, finding solace in words long before she could fully grasp the depths of her emotions. Poetry became her refuge—her voice when spoken words felt too heavy to carry. Through heartbreak, trauma, and quiet battles, she poured her soul onto the page, turning pain into poetry.

Longing to bring her poetry beyond the written word, Belinda began performing spoken word pieces on Instagram. Her raw, unfiltered emotions struck a deep chord with others, sparking an overwhelming response that led to Breathing in Broken Spaces, her debut poetry collection—a reflection on pain, resilience, and the search for meaning in fractured places. Each piece carries the weight of loss, the ache of healing, and the quiet strength that emerges from suffering.

This is only the beginning. Belinda continues to explore themes of heartbreak, trauma, healing, and self-discovery, giving voice to emotions often left unspoken. Through her work, she hopes to reach those who feel broken, unseen, or lost—reminding them that even in darkness, light remains, a voice can be reclaimed, and a story still waits to be told.

You can follow her journey on Instagram @bell.d.poet, where she shares poetry and spoken word performances—creating a space for connection, reflection, and healing.